FREE

'Those who e...
supernatural powers find it hard
to remain sceptical'
The Independent

'I am quite convinced she has
certain remarkable powers'
The Mail on Sunday

FREE
YOUR
MIND
A Little Book of Life

BETTY SHINE

HarperCollins*Publishers*

HarperCollins*Publishers*
77-85 Fulham Palace Road
Hammersmith, London W6 8JB
www.**fire**and**water**.com

Published by HarperCollins*Publishers* 1999
1 3 5 7 9 8 6 4 2

Material extracted from *A Mind of Your Own*
published by HarperCollins*Publishers* 1998

Copyright © Betty Shine 1998, 1999

Betty Shine asserts the moral right to
be identified as the author of this work.

ISBN 0 00 653183 0

Cover photographs © Telegraph Colour Library

Printed and bound in Great Britain by
Woolnough Bookbinding Limited, Irthlingborough

INTRODUCTION

When my book *A Mind of Your Own* was published, it became obvious very quickly from the huge amount of mail I received daily that people hated to leave behind the comfort and advice in that book when they left home.

So the pocket book *Clear Your Mind* was launched, containing 75 extracts from the parent book. This too was an immediate success – and not only amongst readers of *A Mind of Your Own* – and it became obvious that another little book would be warmly welcomed. I have called this new book *Free Your Mind,* which evokes that feeling of freedom we all seek in our hectic lives.

I have been especially delighted to receive letters from teenagers who have found *Clear Your Mind* so helpful. I hope that *Free Your Mind* will also give them the comfort they need at this challenging time of life.

Whatever your age, these books get to the heart of the problem and bring common sense and logic into our lives when we most need it. They will also enable you to counsel others in distress. Try simply holding the book for a few seconds and then opening it – you will be amazed how pertinent the page you open will be!

If you would like more detail on the contents of this book and accompanying visualisations, you will find them in the parent book *A Mind of Your Own*.

Betty Shine

ABUSE

Whatever you do, stamp out abuses,
and love those who love you.

VOLTAIRE
1694–1778

〜〜

No one should have to tolerate abuse of any kind, and there can be no excuse for this abominable practice. Mental or physical abuse to any living thing should never go unchallenged or unreported. Never condone this behaviour. Even a bystander *can* take action.

There is no excuse for abuse.

〜〜

ADDICTION

*In a consumer society there are
inevitably two kinds of slaves:
the prisoners of addiction
and the prisoners of envy.*

IVAN ILLICH
1926–

Nearly everyone, at some time in their lives, becomes addicted to something. It can be alcohol, tobacco, television, sports, chocolate... The power of the mind can, eventually, help you to conquer addiction. Never give up. You can do it.

Addiction is an affliction.

ANXIETY

*When you're lying awake with a dismal
headache, and repose is taboo'd by anxiety,
I conceive you may use any language you
choose to indulge in, without impropriety.*

W. S. GILBERT
1836–1911

For some people being in a state of permanent anxiety is the norm, having never experienced peace of mind. However, minds that are fully occupied don't have time to indulge in anxiety and are usually healthier for it.

**Anxiety is counterproductive –
I don't need it.**

〜〜

BITTERNESS

Teach us delight in simple things,
And mirth that has no bitter springs;
Forgiveness free of evil done,
And love to all men 'neath the sun!

RUDYARD KIPLING
1865–1936

Bitterness is a difficult emotion to deal with. Memories invade the privacy of your thoughts and the pain never seems to go away. Take a pen and paper and write everything down as it comes into your head; when you have finished, *do not read it through,* or you will be feeding it back into your mind. Place your notes in an old tin in the sink, put a match to them and watch them burn, knowing that your bitter thoughts are being reduced to ashes.

Bitterness sears the soul.

BURDENS

With aching hands and bleeding feet
We dig and heap, lay stone on stone;
We bear the burden and the heat
Of the long day, and wish 'twere done.
Not till the hours of light return,
All we have built do we discern.

MATTHEW ARNOLD
1822–1888

Burdens of any kind can cause havoc with your lifestyle, and particularly with your health. Although the mind and body can take an enormous amount of pressure, everyone has their breaking point. The art of dealing with any burden is to despatch it as quickly as possible. Live your life to the full. Surround yourself with friends and fill your life with laughter.

I do not have to walk this path alone.

〜〜

CAREER

Weary with toil, I haste to my bed,
The dear repose for limbs with travel tired;
But then begins a journey in my head
To work my mind, when body's
work's expired.

WILLIAM SHAKESPEARE
1564–1616

To be successful in a chosen career is invigorating and exciting. Every day is a challenge. But no matter how successful you may be, it is always wise to be aware of the pitfalls. Be mindful of your health at all times, and hold on to your integrity, for without it you are nothing.

Success is nothing without friends.

৵~

CAREFREE

The learn'd is happy nature to explore,
The fool is happy that he knows no more.

ALEXANDER POPE
1688–1744

You must find time, on a regular basis, to indulge in being carefree. This exhilarating pastime is essential for your health. Once you have experienced the freedom and the sense of belonging to nature, I guarantee you will become hooked. Years of being worn down with pressure and responsibility will vanish and your mind will become clear, enabling you to see the real beauty around you.

Everything is possible.

⌒⌒

CARERS

Life may change, but it may fly not;
Hope may vanish, but can die not;
Truth be veiled, but still it burneth;
Love repulsed, – but it returneth!

PERCY BYSSHE SHELLEY
1792–1822

The job of caring is usually thrust upon individuals. If the patient is a member of the family, the carer is usually pressurised into believing that it is their duty to take on the burden of becoming nurse/housekeeper. But under pressure, their own health may also suffer. If you are a carer, please seek help. If you are not a carer but can find some time to spare – even if only a couple of hours a week – see if you can help.

I shall help every day.

CHEATING

I to my perils
Of cheat and charmer
Came clad in armour
By stars benign.

A. E. HOUSMAN
1859–1936

Cheating is loathsome and deprives
the cheat of integrity. Stealing
something you had no right to have
can only bring misery. Only achieving
your goals on your own merit will bring
happiness and fulfilment and the
knowledge that you can
survive alone.

**My achievements will always be a
product of my own unique ability.**

~~

CLAIRVOYANCE

Lives of great men all remind us
We can make our lives sublime,
And, departing, leave behind us
Footprints in the sands of time.

HENRY WADSWORTH LONGFELLOW
1807–1882

Clairvoyance is the ability to see clearly into the future. A talented clairvoyant can warn of dangers if it is obvious that you are taking a wrong path. In my experience, though, people only want to hear about the positive things. Your own intuition is the finest clairvoyance you can have – you will be amazed at how right you can be.

I will have faith in my own instincts.

CLASS

Bow, bow, ye lower middle classes!
Bow, bow, ye tradesmen, bow, ye masses.

W. S. GILBERT
1836–1911

Unfortunately, a class system exists in nearly every country in the world, but as individuals it should not present a problem. Class, as I see it, should be about dignity, no matter what race or creed. We can all attain it. To be dignified is not to be blind, it is knowing how to protect your image in the correct manner and keep your self-respect.

I am a class act – and hard to follow.

〜〜

Colour

And life is colour and warmth and light
And a striving evermore for these;
And he is dead, who will not fight;
And who dies fighting has increase.
The fighting man shall from the sun
Take warmth, and life from the
glowing earth.

JULIAN GRENFELL
1888–1915

When you go out, look around you and wonder at the changing colours of the seasons. Do you really notice them, or do you walk around blind to the beauty that surrounds you? Add colour to your home to make it warm and welcoming. Even adding colour to your outfit by adding a bright scarf or tie will give you a more joyous and healthy existence.

The colours of my life must glow with iridescent beauty.

～〜

COMMUNICATION

*To do good and to communicate
forget not.*

THE BIBLE, HEBREWS

The ability to communicate is society's life-support system. Without it, we are lost. The voice is, and always will be, the finest way to communicate. Although there has to be a place in the modern world for machines, especially in business, do not make the mistake of totally replacing that very special piece of communications equipment – the voice.

The art of conversation is a gift – I must use it.

〜〜

CONCEIT

Words are the tokens current and accepted
for conceits, as moneys are for values.

FRANCIS BACON
1561–1626

Conceit is an extremely unpleasant trait. Arrogance of any kind is undesirable but self-love is repugnant in the extreme. It is totally different from loving and being comfortable with oneself. Conceit stems from such a lack of knowledge about oneself that the personality is tricked into thinking it is in some way exalted.

I want my life to be complete. I must rid myself of conceit.

〜〜

CONCENTRATION

*Depend upon it, Sir, when a man knows
he is to be hanged in a fortnight, it
concentrates his mind wonderfully.*

SAMUEL JOHNSON
1709–1784

〜✿〜

From infants to adults, lack of concentration is often caused by boredom. On the other hand, we are totally focused when we are enthusiastic about something. Talented teachers can catch the imagination of their pupils and induce concentration in even the most reluctant individual.

Enthusiasm for life will stimulate my concentration.

CONSCIENCE

*Labour to keep alive in your breast that
little spark of celestial fire, called
conscience.*

GEORGE WASHINGTON
1732–1799

Common sense combined with a healthy conscience is a good balance, resulting in a state that enhances not only our lives but the lives of others. Temptation is never very far away. But is it really worth giving into it, when you'll have it on your conscience for the rest of your life?

I must heed my conscience at all times.

CRYING

When we are born we cry that we are come
To this great stage of fools.

WILLIAM SHAKESPEARE
1564–1616

Crying is the most therapeutic thing
that you can do. If the cause of your
despair is especially tragic, then continue
to cleanse your soul, for that is what
crying is – a cleansing of the soul.

Cry – cleanse – heal.

DANGER

Danger, the spur of all great minds.

GEORGE CHAPMAN
c.1559–1634

～

Children love danger. Most of them court it because it is exciting. Some children never grow up and as adults still seek out the danger in life. If the results are positive and eventually turn them into human beings with a touch of the child within, then it is fine. But don't be irresponsible and leave others to pick up the pieces.

I must be responsible for my own actions and think of others while doing so.

〜〜

DESTINY

Sow an act, and you reap a habit.
Sow a habit and you reap a character.
Sow a character, and you reap a destiny.

CHARLES READE
1814–1884

Throughout your life you will dance from path to path, sampling delights and miseries and forming a character. You are destined to become whatever you become and, through your becoming, you will arrive at your destination. Think carefully every step of the way, because your destiny is in your hands.

My destiny will be of my own making.

〜〜

DEVIL

The Devil watches all opportunities.

WILLIAM CONGREVE
1670–1729

❦❦

The devil is within all of us. Do not allow this energy to interfere with your life. Surround yourself with flowers and glowing colours and these negative energies will retreat. You can also eliminate them with positive thoughts of love for life. Thoughts must always be disciplined, but emotions must never be stifled. Create a balance.

I will fight the devil within for I have so much love to give.

∽∼

DISCIPLINE

*The discipline of colleges and universities
is in general contrived, not for the benefit
of the students, but for the interest, or
more properly speaking, for the ease of
the masters.*

SAMUEL SMILES
1812–1904

∽∾

If your children are badly behaved in public then they are not receiving enough discipline at home. If they appear to be browbeaten then the discipline could be bordering on abuse. Happy, carefree children who have respect for their parents are more likely to be receiving moderate amounts of discipline intertwined with love. By monitoring your children's behaviour, you could also learn a lot about yourself.

I will discipline with humour, which will lighten everyone's life.

DIVORCE

Seal then this bill of my divorce to all.

JOHN DONNE
c.1571–1631

Divorce can be a terrible thing. It can also be viewed as a positive opportunity. If you can, keep bitterness within the confines of friends and family. Of course you want to rant and rave, and it will probably keep you sane, but it rarely solves anything and strangers will never understand your anguish. Only your nearest and dearest can help you with that.

If there has to be divorce, then I will come out of it with my sanity and my health.

EGO

For the sake of a few fine imaginative or domestic passages, are we to be bullied into a certain philosophy engendered in the whims of an egoist?

JOHN KEATS
1795–1821

If you have an over-inflated ego and are puffed up with your own self-importance, do something about it. Look at the faces around you whilst you are expounding your theories or 'doing your stuff' – I think you will be surprised. Egotism is curable but takes effort. If you make that effort you might find that you make many more friends.

Egocentric personalities are a bore.

〜〜

EMOTION

Poetry is the spontaneous overflow
of powerful feelings:
it takes its origin from emotion
recollected in tranquillity.

WILLIAM WORDSWORTH
1770–1850

Our emotional reactions to situations throughout life are triggered by previous experiences. A look, word or action can bring to the surface both happy and unhappy memories and the response can sometimes be quite unexpected and mystifying. Do not allow negative emotions to affect your health – they cause havoc with the immune system, so beware!

My emotions are part of my being, but they must be controlled.

〜〜

ENTERTAINING

Lay aside life-harming heaviness,
And entertain a cheerful disposition.

WILLIAM SHAKESPEARE
1564–1616

In your private life it is wise not to mix too many personalities when it is your turn to play host. Entertaining will be a pleasure if everyone has at least one common interest. But when you *do* have to entertain someone with whom you are incompatible, make the effort to be pleasant – you want to make it a successful occasion for all concerned.

Good manners must always prevail.

ENVY

If at times my eyes are lenses
through which the brain explores
constellations of feeling
my ears yielding like swinging doors
admit princes to the corridors
into the mind, do not envy me.
I have a beast on my back.

KEITH DOUGLAS
1920–1944

Envy can poison the mind and corrupt the soul, causing disruptive behaviour, violence and death. Every day there is evidence of the evil that it brings into our lives, and the tragedy is that it can start in childhood. Never covet this emotion – it can lead only to disaster.

I will not envy others. A healthy, happy nature is worth its weight in gold.

EXCESS

The best things carried to excess are wrong.

CHARLES CHURCHILL
1731–1764

If you love something or someone, you will inevitably take things to excess. This behaviour is not healthy if it continues. Self-satisfaction can become habitual and will eventually lead to your downfall. Excess can only be tolerated a little at a time – you must know when to slow down or stop.

Excessive behaviour can lead to disaster. Be careful!

FAMILIARITY

Yea, even mine own familiar friend,
whom I trusted:
who did also eat of my bread, hath
laid great wait for me.

BOOK OF COMMON PRAYER
1662

~ ~

Having friends and family with whom you can be familiar gives a feeling of belonging, of knowing that you are part of something bigger. It is, above all, a warm, cosy feeling, like warming your toes by the fire. However, if you are not sure whether you can trust someone, then do not open yourself up to them; keep quiet until they have proved themselves.

Familiarity can breed contempt or it can be a blessing – only time will tell.

〜〜

GIFTS

Every good gift and every perfect gift is from above, and cometh down from the Father of lights, with whom is no variableness, neither shadow of turning.

THE BIBLE, JAMES

If you have been born with gifts, do not waste them. They are a blessed mixture of all the things you have acquired in past lives, born out of hard work and courage. They are your birthright. Work at them, add to them; the more difficult a situation becomes, the more character-building it is. It will be worth it.

I will not quit.

GIVING

I am not in the giving vein today.

WILLIAM SHAKESPEARE
1564–1616

❧❧

If you are a born giver, then inevitably the takers will latch on to you throughout your life. The secret is to know when to stop giving. This will only come through experience, and even then it is difficult. Try to strengthen your mind so that it becomes easier to say 'No'.

'No' must become a regular part of my vocabulary.

～～

GRATITUDE

*One single grateful thought raised to heaven
is the most perfect prayer.*

G. E. LESSING
1729–1781

If you are offered help but there is a danger that the helper wants you to be forever grateful to boost their ego, perhaps you should refuse the offer of help and seek it elsewhere. People should assist without expectancy of reward – verbal thanks should be the end of the gratitude. When you do return a favour, do so without obligation.

I will refuse help from anyone who seeks to boost their ego by giving favours.

GRIEF

Farewell sadness
Good day sadness
You are inscribed in the lines of the ceiling.

PAUL ÉLUARD
1895–1952

‏〜❦〜‎

Tears shed by those who are grieving
are the only blessed relief when locked
in an anguished embrace of memories
of things that were meant to be and
words that were never said. Because we
are all unique, the time to relinquish
the cloak of despair and 'look to the
future' will be different for everyone.

**The act of grieving, when burnt out,
will bring its own kind of peace.**

HARMONY

The day becomes more solemn and serene
When noon is past – there is a harmony
In autumn, and a lustre in its sky,
Which through the summer is not heard
or seen,
As if it could not be, as if it had not been!

PERCY BYSSHE SHELLEY
1792–1822

Harmony in your life is essential. It will elevate your spirit and bring peace to every fibre of your being. If you cannot attain it in your work or home, try to find a secret place where you can relax, if only for a few minutes every day. If all else fails, just close your eyes and picture yourself floating through the air.

I must bring harmony into my life. I will succeed!

HEARTBREAK

Nor feel the heart-break in the heart of things.

WILFRED GIBSON
1878–1962

If you are suffering heartbreak, someone, somewhere, is going through the same agonies as you. Keep your mind and body intact by releasing the grief: scream, cry, wail and sob. Above all, do not suffer alone. Life still goes on and you will have to deal with it somehow.

When I need help, need to speak to a friend, need someone to hold me close, I only have to ask.

～～

HUMOUR

*The most perfect humour and irony is
generally quite unconscious.*

SAMUEL BUTLER
1835–1902

〜〜

Humour should be at the very centre of every family circle. Children should be encouraged to laugh at themselves and to see the funny side of every situation. Life, love and laughter should be your motto. Laughter is the beginning of all healing – without it we are lost.

Humour is wonderful. I am going to encourage more of it in my life.

〜〜

IGNORANCE

I pity his ignorance and despise him.

CHARLES DICKENS
1812–1870

There are many people who blight our lives by being ignorant. Insensitive, rude, shallow and superficial, they bruise everyone who displeases them, leaving behind a trail of broken spirits. They are unhappy people who need to look seriously at their state of mind. If you recognise yourself, do something about it – people will despise you for ever if you don't.

Nobody is born unpleasant. It takes dedication – not something to be proud of.

INSPIRATION

*Genius is one per cent inspiration,
ninety-nine per cent perspiration.*

THOMAS ALVA EDISON
1847–1931

~⦿~

It is a tragedy that the world today values noise above the sanctuary of silence, for it is only there that you will find the key to inspiration. If you are the kind of person who inspires others, remember that you have only been given knowledge in order to pass it on for the good of others and not simply to impress or to bolster your ego.

**Inspirational thought is a gift
I must never abuse.**

෨෨

LETHARGY

This apoplexy is, as I take it, a kind of lethargy, an't please your lordship; a kind of sleeping in the blood, a whoreson tingling.

WILLIAM SHAKESPEARE
1564–1616

Lethargy is a great time waster and a strain on your health. Are you eating sensibly? Bad eating habits mean that you may be deficient in vitamins and minerals. Are you getting enough sleep? Are you working so hard that you can't relax even when you have time off? Or are you having a difficult relationship with someone? You must sort out the cause.

When I feel lethargic I will check out every aspect of my life.

〜〜

MAGIC

When I came back from Lyonnesse
With magic in my eyes,
All marked with mute surmise
My radiance rare and fathomless,
When I came back from Lyonnesse
With magic in my eyes!

THOMAS HARDY
1840–1928

Why look for magic to brighten up your life when you can conjure up a bit of magic for yourself? All you need to do is paint a picture with your mind, enhance and strengthen it daily, and you will soon be living with magic. Your imagery can take you into the realms of fact or fantasy.

Magic will become part of my life from now on.

MIND

Idleness is only the refuge of weak minds.

EARL OF CHESTERFIELD
1694–1773

As the computer needs electricity to activate it, the brain needs mind power. The more positive you are the more powerful you become. Negativity weakens the mind, body and spirit, and though it would be hard to banish negative thought altogether, never indulge in it for more than five minutes at a time.

Positivity renews.
Negativity destroys.

⤸⤹

MIRACLES

By the time a man gets well into the seventies his continued existence is a mere miracle.

ROBERT LOUIS STEVENSON
1850–1894

Miracles do happen. In all the healing practices – whatever they may be – there are people whose caring is enough to give a bit of *oomph* to the process. If you can also do your bit, then your particular miracle could be nearer than you think.

I have to take the first step before I can expect a miracle.

～❦～

MYSTICISM

*I have often admired the mystical
way of Pythagoras, and the secret magic
of numbers.*

SIR THOMAS BROWNE
1605–1682

∽ ∼

Some mysticism can appear to be fantasy, but mystics interact all the time with other dimensions and know the reality of them. Without mysticism, unbelievers would have to find some other target for their prejudice, while the lives of believers would seem futile without that little bit of magic they know is readily available for the asking.

I will never have expectations of others, only myself.

NIGHTMARES

*History is a nightmare
from which I am trying to awake.*

JAMES JOYCE
1882–1941

Nightmares come from a troubled mind. Negative emotions cripple your mind, so write down the things you hate and fear, then go through the list eliminating them one by one. If you take the time to think through your life and sort out the problems, your nightmares will gradually fade away.

I will not allow my life to become a living nightmare.

PEACE

Over all the mountain tops is peace.

JOHANN WOLFGANG VON GOETHE
1749–1832

〜〜

The path to peace is a maze
through which we stumble and fall;
yet in the seeking, an awareness of
our own self-worth will emerge and we
will learn that the peace we seek is
within us. The journey will be hard but
the rewards are great, for without peace
we have nothing.

**If changes are necessary to find the
peace within, I will make them.**

〜〜

PHENOMENA

Language was not powerful enough to describe the infant phenomenon.

CHARLES DICKENS
1812–1870

It can be very difficult to come to terms with paranormal phenomena. Incidents are initiated from other dimensions, to create and make an impression to achieve a goal. It could be in healing, in mediumship, or in meditation. The paranormal does exist, and maybe one day something special will happen to you.

An open mind is the key to the secrets of the universe.

∽∾

PHOBIAS

Because the road is rough and long,
Shall we despise the skylark's song?

ANNE BRONTË
1820–1849

Phobias come from a deep-rooted fear
of life that impinges itself on a particular
subject or object – they are the effect, not
the cause. Rid yourself of the fear in your
subconscious, face it and learn from it,
and you will find that the phobia
will disappear.

**Abolish fear and the phobias
will disappear.**

PRIORITIES

The heavens themselves, the planets,
and this centre
Observe degree, priority and place,
Insisture, course, proportion, season, form,
Office, and custom, in all line of order.

WILLIAM SHAKESPEARE
1564–1616

To have order in your life, you must get your priorities right. It is usually quite easy to recognise the order in which they should be placed, but where emotions are involved, mistakes can be made which lead to misunderstandings and lost friendships. Write down what you consider to be your priorities. As you review the list, put those which produce the strongest reaction in you at the top.

I will take time to get my priorities right.

REPUTATION

Indeed the idols I have loved so long
Have done my credit in this world
much wrong:
Have drown'd my glory in a shallow cup
And sold my reputation for a song.

EDWARD FITZGERALD
1809–1883

It is absolutely essential that you safeguard your reputation. No matter what status you may have in life, having a good reputation will bring you the respect of others. Opportunities will come your way because people trust you with their confidences. Above all, you will be known to have honour.

If something instinctively feels wrong, I shall keep away from it.

෨෩

SELF

The spirit is the true self.

CICERO
106–43 BC

Meditation is the easiest way to communicate with the self. Having a mirror image of yourself can be painful, but once you know your true self you are better able to deal with personal problems. Above all, *to thine own self be true*. This is not as easy as it sounds, but is well worth the effort.

Know thyself.

〜〜

SELF-ESTEEM

Oft-times nothing profits more
Than self-esteem, grounded on just
and right
Well managed.

JOHN MILTON
1608–1674

～❧～

If you have self-esteem you
can manage your life, secure in the
knowledge that your intuitive words
and actions are serving you well. It is not
always easy to hold on to self-esteem
when everything about us is falling
apart, but it is at these times that we
need it most, reducing tensions and
enabling us to think clearly.

My self-esteem is high – I feel good!

༄༅

SELF-IMPORTANCE

*You may think that you are important,
but there are billions of people out there
who don't give a damn*

BETTY SHINE

〜∾

People who are self-important are irritating, to say the least. They should look around and study those who are successful human beings, who have caring and loving relationships with friends and family. Self-importance isolates you from people, until friends become a thing of the past.

Self-importance is an embarrassment.

〜〜

SELF-INDULGENCE

The way in which the man of genius rules is by persuading an efficient minority to coerce an indifferent and self-indulgent majority.

SIR JAMES FITZJAMES STEPHEN
1829–1894

Self-indulgence is a crime against yourself, giving in to the weaker side of your character because you are too lazy to do otherwise. Self-indulgent people are difficult to live with and difficult to work with, as they are unable, for whatever reason, to think of anyone but themselves. The only way a self-indulgent person can change is if *they* want to.

I do not have to dance to the tune of self-indulgent people.

SENSITIVITY

I shook the habit off
Entirely and for ever, and again
In Nature's presence stood, as now I stand,
A sensitive being, a creative soul.

WILLIAM WORDSWORTH
1770–1850

Sensitivity can be a curse as well as a blessing. If you are too sensitive you will find life difficult until you have learnt to deal with it. Do not try to change others to suit your sensitive nature – the remedy lies within *you*. There is life out there for you, and you will succeed.

If I am hurt, I will ride the crest of the wave.

❧❧

SEXUAL HARASSMENT

The soft, unhappy sex.

MRS APHRA BEHN
1640–1689

❧❧

Sexual harassment is a crime, and the perpetrator should be dealt with immediately. There can be no excuse for anyone who invades another person's space in this way. Protect yourself by sharing your experiences with a counsellor – do not under any circumstances keep this experience to yourself. The more people who know, the safer you will be.

I will protect myself at all costs and fight for my rights.

〜〜

SHOUTING

Every man shouting in proportion to the amount of his subscription.

R. S. SURTEES
1805–1864

~~~

Shouting really is a waste of time, because your message becomes a blurred noise and the impact that you wish to make is lost. The only time that shouting is justified is when you are warning someone of danger or participating in sport or games that induce high spirits. Otherwise curb the noise, calm down, and get your point home with intelligent conversation.

I will re-educate myself not to shout.

SHOWERS

She said no more and as she turned away
there was a bright glimpse of the rosy glow
of her neck, and from her ambrosial head of
hair a heavenly fragrance wafted;
her dress flowed right to her feet, and in
her walk it showed,
she was in truth a goddess.

VIRGIL
70–19 BC

When the day is done and we return home tired and crumpled, there is nothing as refreshing as a shower. Standing with the warm cascading water caressing your body, you can feel the tensions evaporate, and peace is restored. It imitates the effect of nature's rain showers – that feeling of cleanliness as dust and grime are washed away and natural colours regain their healthy sheen.

Refreshed and revitalised, I am ready to face the world again.

SILENCE

Under all speech that is good for anything there lies a silence that is better. Silence is deep as Eternity; speech is shallow as Time.

THOMAS CARLYLE
1795–1881

〜〜

Complete silence is very necessary for your health. The mind, body and spirit all need silence to rejuvenate and regenerate the whole. Make a special time every day for your silent hour – it will change your life.

I must always make time for silence in my life.

〜〜

SOBBING

Life is made up of sobs, sniffles, and smiles,
with sniffles predominating.

O. HENRY
1862–1910

～～

When emotions are high, sobbing can be the end result of a long crying session; shock can cause immediate sobbing, as can persistent pain. The body, no longer able to retain the pressure, causes a reaction that releases the pent-up emotions, so in short doses sobbing can be good for you. If it continues, you must make the effort to curb it slowly until it ends.

No matter how bad things are, nothing lasts for ever.

～～

SOLITUDE

For oft, when on my couch I lie
In vacant or in pensive mood,
They flash upon that inward eye
Which is the bliss of solitude;
And then my heart with pleasure fills,
And dances with the daffodils.

WILLIAM WORDSWORTH
1770–1850

Solitude is a must for a writer, because any kind of noise or interruption can cause one to lose the train of thought, and to an author lost words can cause great sadness. There are many reasons for seeking solitude, but remember to keep a balance in your life. No matter how important it is to you, do not shut out friends and family. There is a time and a place for everything.

In my solitude I will touch my soul.

SOUL

Let knowledge grow from more to more,
But more of reverence in us dwell;
That mind and soul, according well,
May make one music as before.

ALFRED, LORD TENNYSON
1809–1892

I believe that the mind *is* the soul. Whatever your views, I am sure that you will agree that it is very warming to think that we do have a soul and that it will continue to protect and shield us from the negative energies that exist in all dimensions.

My soul dictates the kind of person I am.

〜〜

SPITE

Only take this rule along,
Always to advise her wrong;
And reprove her when she's right;
She may then grow wise for spite.

JONATHAN SWIFT
1667–1745

Spitefulness is cruel and unnecessary, and underlines the ignorance and low self-esteem of the perpetrator. People disappear in droves when faced with spite, as they simply cannot handle this vindictive trait – and there is no reason why they should have to. If you are a victim, walk away from it, because you will never win.

I must protect myself from spite by walking away.

SYMBOLISM

We are symbols, and inhabit symbols.

RALPH WALDO EMERSON
1803–1882

〜〜

We are initiated into symbolism from birth, mainly through the religious beliefs of our parents. In the absence of religion, symbols come via sports, hobbies or family traditions. With our own private symbols we make major decisions, hold on to the image for support when times are bad, and hail them as our saviours when the good times reappear.

Symbolism is the positive spark that ignites the mind, to seek and find.

～～

TEMPERAMENT

A being breathing thoughtful breath,
A traveller betwixt life and death;
The reason firm, the temperate will,
Endurance, foresight, strength and skill;
A perfect woman, nobly planned,
To warn, to comfort, and command;
And yet a spirit still, and bright
With something of angelic light.

WILLIAM WORDSWORTH
1770–1850

If you have a friend with an even temperament, then count your blessings. It is wonderful to know that you have someone in whom you can confide. Count your blessings too if *you* have an even temperament, because you will experience more peace, contentment and goodwill than those who have not.

I will endeavour to even out my temperament.

〜〜

THOUGHT

This gray spirit yearning in desire
To follow knowledge like a sinking star,
Beyond the utmost bound of human
thought.

ALFRED, LORD TENNYSON
1809–1892

⤚⤙

We need time to think. Our thoughts are the most precious thing we have; they trigger the imagination, enabling us to enhance and bring to life hitherto unseen images. It is imperative that we take the time to think, for without thought we will find ourselves in a grey place.

I cannot reach a conclusion without proper thought.

༄༅

THREATS

Breathing out threatenings and slaughter.

THE BIBLE, ACTS OF THE APOSTLES

Ignorance and an inferiority complex are the main reasons for people indulging in threatening behaviour. Unable to converse adequately, they torment their victims instead. If you are threatened and you are able to walk away from the situation, do so. If you see someone else being threatened, get help.

If I can walk away, I shall do so.

෴෴

TRAGEDY

The bad end unhappily, the good unluckily.
That is what tragedy means.

TOM STOPPARD
1937–

∽∼

Some people can go through life without experiencing one single tragedy, while others have tragedies heaped upon them, and there seems to be no rhyme or reason why this should be. We try to find some common factor that links the tragedies, to make sense of the grief, but in the end we have to live with the aftermath. Go with the flow of your emotions – the river of life will eventually carry you into calmer waters.

We are a small cog in a large wheel, and it must keep turning

TROUBLE

No stranger to trouble myself
I am learning to care for the unhappy.

VIRGIL
70–19 BC

A troubled mind will always find trouble, as it is never far away. The root cause of many illnesses is worrying about imaginary problems that may never materialise. There is an old saying, 'Never trouble trouble, 'til trouble troubles you.' I think this should be imprinted on our minds at all times.

In future, trouble can take a back seat. I want to be happy.

∾∾

UNLUCKY

Therefore, since the world has still
Much good, but much less good than ill,
And while the sun and moon endure
Luck's a chance, but trouble's sure,
I'd face it as a wise man would,
And train for ill and not for good.

A. E. HOUSMAN
1859–1936

Once you have the feeling that you were born unlucky, you have sealed your fate, because you have created a blueprint in your mind that will stay with you forever. To achieve a positive approach to life and cancel it out, tell yourself you make your own luck, and by doing so change the blueprint – then you can get on with living a full and happy life.

There is a way out, but there have to be changes in my mental attitude to life.

UNREASONABLE

The reasonable man adapts himself to the world: the unreasonable one persists in trying to adapt the world to himself. Therefore all progress depends upon the unreasonable man.

GEOGRE BERNARD SHAW
1856–1950

There can be no excuse for unreasonable behaviour. It is disruptive and adds unnecessary stress to already difficult situations. Fortunately, persistently unreasonable people are eventually cold-shouldered by friends and family. It is far better to keep our self-respect and resist the temptation to stoop to their level.

Persistent unreasonable behaviour is inexcusable.

WEAK-WILLED

Oh, Vanity of vanities!
How wayward the decrees of Fate are;
How very weak the very wise,
How very small the very great are!

WILLIAM MAKEPEACE THACKERAY
1811–1863

❧❧

Very few admit to being weak-willed because it needs positive effort to combat it, and laziness is inherent in people with this weakness in their character. The biggest problem is that they find it easier to say *yes* than *no* and then go through hell, fire and water to carry out the wishes of others.

I will say no to idiotic suggestions, and choose my own positive path.

〜〜

WEALTH

Let not ambition mock their useful toil,
Their homely joys, and destiny obscure;
Nor grandeur hear with a disdainful smile,
The short and simple annals of the poor.

THOMAS GRAY
1716–1771

I would place health, happiness and wealth in that order. If you are healthy, you can work towards becoming wealthy; if you are happy and healthy, your task will be more pleasurable. But wealth alone, though it can give one the creature comforts, has very little going for it if the stress of managing it makes you miserable and ill.

My health and happiness are more important than wealth.

༄༅

WORLD

You daren't handle high explosives; but you're all ready to handle honesty and truth and justice and the whole duty of man, and kill one another at that game. What a country! What a world!

GEORGE BERNARD SHAW
1856–1950

The beauties of this planet are usually overshadowed by the stories of the persecution of its inhabitants around the world. Everyone who loves this planet that is our home should protect it and its inhabitants to the best of their ability. We should not strive for personal riches, but for the chance to live out our lives in peace.

I will help the world to help itself.

〜〜

Yarns

I must go down to the sea again, to the
vagrant gypsy life,
To the gull's way and the whale's way
where the wind's like a whetted knife;
And all I ask is a merry yarn from a
laughing fellow-rover,
And quiet sleep and a sweet dream when
the long trick's over.

JOHN MASEFIELD
1878–1967

I am always amazed at the inventiveness of story-tellers. Their imagination knows no bounds, as adults and children alike sit spellbound as the stories unfold. What a gift! So if you have the gift of the story-teller, enhance it, and brighten up all of our lives.

There is always a bit of wisdom in a yarn. Look for it.

～～

YEARNING

Give me your tired, your poor,
Your huddled masses yearning to
breathe free . . .

EMMA LAZARUS
1849–1887

We all have strong emotional longings at some time in our lives, but when the hunger never ceases it is time to move on. Yearning can be a simple hankering or a terrible craving, therefore it must be controlled before it gets out of hand. There is a life waiting for you – find it and get rid of the yearning that is threatening to ruin your future.

I will turn the yearning into a learning experience.

ZEST

I love all that thou lovest,
Spirit of delight:
The fresh Earth in new leaves dressed,
And the starry night;
Autumn evening, and the morn
When the golden mists are born.

PERCY BYSSHE SHELLEY
1792–1822

I hope this book will give you the zest to live your life to the full. *Zest.* What a wonderful word! Invigorating, exciting, and full of joy. If you spend the rest of your life working towards this goal you will have fun. If you have already experienced this feeling, hold that dream and never let it go, for one day it will return, perhaps when you least expect it.

I will look for the zest in life and make my dreams come true.

～～

If you wish to receive distant healing,
books, tapes or teaching brochures,
please write to:

Betty Shine,
P.O. Box 1009,
Hassocks,
West Sussex,
BN6 8XS

Please enclose a stamped addressed
envelope for a reply. Thank you.

About the author

Betty Shine is known worldwide for her powers as a medium and healer. She is the author of a number of bestselling books, including her autobiography *My Life as a Medium*. A former opera singer, Betty has been a medium, healer and hypnotherapist for 25 years, and a vitamin and mineral therapist for over 40 years.

'The world's number one healer'
The Sun